For Girls ONLY

A Loving Appeal for Modesty in an Immodest World

Sheila Stewart Doom

ISBN 1-56632-130-1

Printed in the United States of America.

Preface

This book has been written with the young teenage girl in mind. Undoubtedly, however, others will read it, and among these some will interpret what is written as setting forth standards much too binding for a Christian who has been set free by the grace of God. To these dear saints in particular, I would ask that the Scriptures be allowed to dictate to the conscience rather than the conscience to the Scriptures.

A fine Christian brother, Jeff Pollard, author of *Modesty and the Public Undressing of America*, introduced his book with these words:

> *Test it by the Scriptures; hold fast to that which is good. If you do not find the studies and conclusions here to be biblical, reject them. Christ's free men should not be bound by the opinions of men. And if you find them to be in harmony to God's Word, bow to His truth and serve Him with joy and gladness.*

My sentiments are the same.

The Apostle Paul wrote to the Galatian believers, "For, brethren, ye have been called unto liberty; only use not liberty for an occasion to the flesh, but by love serve one another." (Galatians 5:13) I trust that this is the same spirit in which I have presented my case for modesty. My sole motive in writing has been to glorify our great and glorious God. In days of apostasy such as we are experiencing, those who name the name of Christ must seek every opportunity to raise high the standard of biblical holiness.

Sheila Stewart Doom
July 2008

3

1

The Issue: Modest Dress

"Do you know what it is like to go to the mall and feel like a freak — like you came from Mars? I'm the only one wearing a skirt — and a long one at that!" The exasperated young lady, all neatly dressed in her cute little jacket and jean skirt, stood in stark contrast to the other girls passing by — their belly buttons exposed, their noses, ears and lips pierced with an array of shiny rings and fake jewels, and their hair tinted purple, pink, and turquoise.

And the young lady wearing the skirt thought she was the freak!

I wish you would pray for me. I have such a hard time keeping my thoughts clean. The thing is, the girls don't help any. They go around exposing so much skin until it's hard for a guy to know where to look and still keep his mind pure. I just wish somebody would tell them.

The young man who had come to me for counseling was perplexed, the young lady intimidated by the pressures to fit in with the crowd.

"Somebody needs to talk to them." I had heard that time and again. "Talk to them." I thought of my oldest granddaughter recently turned sixteen and the talk we had — just the two of us. I tried to cram into our few short moments of intimacy all that was on my heart — the dreams, the warnings, the hopes I have for her. Yet, so much was left unsaid. And with my longings for her, I was reminded of all "my girls" that I have adopted over the years at church, in youth ministry and 25 years of summer camp. They hold a special place in my heart. Yes, it is time to have a talk — about godliness, and modesty, and dress — and well, even about the boys!

Actually, I am even going to let some of my young friends speak for themselves.

First, we are going to talk about what it is to be a Christian. Modesty in dress is part of the *trademark*, or outward sign, that a person is the genuine article — a *real* Christian!

2

The Big Questions

Real Christians have the answers to life's most important questions. These questions and the answers to them clearly set the true Christian apart from those who are simply Christian in name only or make no claim to being one.

Before you rush on to the next chapter, I want you to ask yourself these questions and then think how you would answer them.

1. *Who am I?*
2. *Why am I here — on this planet?*
3. *To whom do I belong?*
4. *Who am I going to please?*

Your answers will have everything to do with what we are going to be talking about in this book.

Who Am I?

Alright, so you are the cutest girl in your class! But that doesn't really answer the question. Surely there have been times when, in a pensive mood, you have asked yourself, "Who am I, really — down underneath the surface where nobody else sees?"

If you attended a public school, you were probably taught that life just happened, that you evolved, that life is just a chance, an accident of nature without rhyme or reason. But, if you know your Bible, you understand that you were in God's mind from the beginning of time and even before that!

Man and woman, male and female — two distinct creations. Woman was God's idea from the beginning, equal to the man in worth, but different in purpose.

> So God created man in his own image, in the image of God created he him; male and female created he them.
> — Genesis 1:27

"In His own image . . ." God did not say this about horses or lions, or any other animal. He created human beings *in His own image* with the ability to love and worship Him in a way none of the rest of His creation can do.

Not only that, but when the time came for you to be conceived, God made you, with your personality, your looks, your own special set of DNA. You are unique, like no other young lady that He ever created before or after! Doesn't that amaze you? You are God's creation!

Why Am I Here?

If God created you *on purpose*, then He has *a purpose* for your life. Why did He create you just the way you are? Have you ever asked yourself, Why am I here?

If you are like most girls your age, there are times you wish you were like someone you admire. You don't like your freckles, or your pug nose (that was my struggle as a young person), or your shyness in front of people. You wish you were prettier or skinnier or more talented like other girls you know. Why did God give you your particular genes that physically make up who you are?

The Bible has the answer.

> *Thou art worthy, O Lord, to receive glory and honour and power: for thou hast created all things, and for thy pleasure they are and were created.* — Revelation 4:11

I will never forget speaking about the Lord with a young man from a rough neighborhood. As I was giving him the gospel, I told him that he had been created to give pleasure to God. His eyes lit up and a look of astonishment flashed across his face. Never before had he heard that his life had purpose.

But you are more than God's creation at birth. If you are a Christian, you are born again and you have been made a new creation by your second birth.

> *Therefore if any man be in Christ, he is a new creature: old things are passed away; behold, all things are become new.* — II Corinthians 5:17

I remember the day when the Lord saved me. Only six years old, I had just started school. It was the Saturday before Easter and Mom started telling me the story of the crucifixion of Jesus Christ. It was an old story that I had heard many times before, but this time was different. The Holy Spirit worked in my heart and showed me Christ dying for me, a six-year-old sinner! I fell on my knees and such a flood of words poured out of my mouth as I prayed for the Lord to forgive my sin and save me! And He did! From that day, I knew the Lord had something for me to do. I refer to it as a *calling*.

> *Even every one that is called by my name: for I have created him for my glory, I have formed him; yea, I have made him. . . . This people have I formed for myself; they shall shew forth my praise.* — Isaiah 43:7, 21

God made you for His glory. He made you to show forth His praise. He made you for His pleasure.

Maybe you have memorized the verse, "Whether therefore ye eat, or drink, or whatsoever ye do, do all to the glory of God." (I Corinthians 10:31)

But what does that mean? Let me put it this way. The Christian's whole purpose in life is to show the world what God is like. Do you realize that God has chosen to display His glory to the world through you, not only through your spirit but also through your body.

Your purpose and my purpose on earth is to glorify God.

To Whom Do I Belong?

How would you answer the question, To whom do I belong? The first answer that comes to the minds of many young girls is, "To my parents." But is that really true? You may have a great mom and dad, but you do not belong to them. You are only loaned to them by God.

Do you belong to yourself? Some girls would be quick to reply, "Yes!" But we do not belong to ourselves.

> *What? know ye not that your body is the temple of the Holy Ghost which is in you, which ye have of God, and ye are not your own? For ye are bought with a price: therefore glorify God in your body, and in your spirit, which are God's.* — I Corinthians 6:19, 20

You are not your own. Through creation *and* through redemption — you were purchased by the precious blood of Christ — you are the possession of Christ. You are not simply His child; you are His possession to do with as He pleases.

Don't you love to belong? That's the hunger in everyone's heart. Think of the awesomeness of belonging to the God of this Universe, the Creator, the One who bought you back from the slave market of sin.

An unusual term in the King James Bible beautifully describes the Christian. The word is "peculiar." The biblical term does not mean "weird," though that is often the way in which we use it today. In the Old Testament *peculiar* has to do with a *treasure* that the owner values above all other things. You can see this in Exodus 19:5 where God says to His people, Israel: "Ye shall be a peculiar treasure unto me."

One writer explained the word "peculiar" this way:

> *The Hebrew word "segullah" signifies God's special jewels, God's proper ones, or God's secret ones, that he keeps in store for himself, and for his own special service and use. . . . God sets as high a value on them as men do upon their treasure.*

If you could once see how precious you are to God as His special (actually that word has the same meaning in the Bible as peculiar), purchased treasure, then you would never again worry about belonging. You do belong to your Creator and Redeemer.

Look again at the sixth chapter of I Corinthians and see what amazing things God has to say about our bodies. Many people teach today that if you are a Christian, only your spirit is important. They believe that it doesn't matter what you do with your body.

But that's not what the Bible says. The Apostle Paul wrote that the "body is. . . for the Lord; and the Lord for the body."

Our body is so important in God's eyes that He is going to resurrect it in the last day.

Also, the Bible says that our "bodies are the members of Christ." This speaks both of His Church and the individuals in the Church. The Scriptures go on to say that our bodies are the temple of the Holy Ghost. My body — *your body* — is the sanctuary where Deity dwells! Wherever we go, the Holy Spirit goes, dwelling within us. Our bodies are the sacred place in which He abides.

Once I was shocked by an article in our local newspaper about vandals breaking into a church building, writing graffiti on the walls and burning hymnbooks and Bibles. That is desecration of the house of God! But this Scripture says that desecrating our bodies is far, far worse. Buildings are really not temples of God. Our bodies are.

Glorifying God in our body and in our spirit rules out all conduct that is not appropriate to the temple of God.

Who Am I Going to Please?

Consider our thoughts so far:
- If I was created to bring pleasure and glory to God . . .
- If I have been saved, redeemed by the precious blood of Christ and therefore am His purchased possession . . .
- If I am now a new creature, with a new Master, a new heart and a new direction . . .
- THEN, who am I going to please?

11

"Sure, I want to please the Lord," you say.

I beg you to search your heart. It's so easy to say one thing, and turn around and do the opposite. For whom are you really living? Friends? Parents? Self? Or can you honestly say that above all else you want to please the One who paid such a high price to redeem you to Himself?

Are you willing to spend your life discovering what pleases God and bringing your life into line with what brings joy, pleasure and glory to His Name? I assure you from experience that it does not happen overnight! We are all selfish individuals by nature. It is only by the workings and promptings of the Holy Spirit that we can change and seek to do God's will rather than our own.

Examine your heart. Can you truthfully say, "Mrs. Sheila, yes, more than anything else in the world I want to please the Lord. More than my friends, more than the young men in my life, more than life itself, I want to please my Lord and Savior."

How do we know what pleases Him? First, we have the Holy Spirit dwelling in our hearts. Jesus Christ went back to heaven and sent us the Holy Spirit to dwell in these *temples of flesh*. The Holy Spirit knows what pleases the Father and He convicts us when we do wrong and fills us with peace and joy when we do right.

Second, if you have come to this place in your life, we can tell you with confidence that you can find God's will for your life in His Word. The child of God who is genuinely born-again agrees with the Psalmist who said, "Great peace have they which love thy law: and nothing shall offend them." (Psalm 119: 165)

My husband loves to tell the story of several students who discovered a veteran missionary reading his Bible. Respectfully, they approached him and asked where he was reading. "I'm just going though the Bible," he replied, "looking for commandments to keep because I love my Lord."

Psalm 40:8 speaks of the Messiah and records Him as saying, "I delight to do thy will, O my God." So will we! When we really love someone, we love doing things that make them happy.

12

"If ye love me, keep my commandments," Jesus told His disciples. To put it simply, we please the Lord by doing what He says. Admittedly, we each must fight against that natural tendency to treat God's Word like a big restaurant buffet, taking what we like and passing by the rest.

3

Keep Thyself Pure

If there is one thing that sets a Christian young person apart from the crowd, it is purity. Take you, for instance. When you purposely set out to keep yourself pure, not only from the outward acts of immorality, but from the inward thoughts of impurity, you are *marked* just as a girl who has been immoral is marked. It will be obvious to everyone.

In the day in which we live, keeping ourselves pure is not easy, is it? TV sit-coms, commercials, billboards, and popular magazines promote an immoral agenda, spewing out filth and if you are not careful, you will find it polluting your mind and life.

Have you ever noticed how an impure image you have seen on

When I was little, my mom told me that she wanted the two of us to wear dresses and skirts instead of pants. Later when the Lord saved me, I understood why my mom wanted us to dress that way. I knew a girl who was much older than me who dressed immodestly. One day I found out she had gotten in trouble and was pregnant. The first thing I thought of was the way she dressed had been a stumbling block. I made up my mind that I was going to keep myself pure and that dressing right was part of it. — O.C.

TV or in a magazine will play itself over and over in your mind, but when you try to remember what the pastor preached on Sunday, you can barely recall one thing? That is the power of sin to taint us. That's why James 1:27 says: "Pure religion and undefiled before God and the Father is this, To visit the fatherless and widows in their affliction, and to keep himself unspotted from the world." God calls young girls to a life of purity. Purity extends from the heart, to the mind, and then to the use of our bodies.

Let's stop here and talk about sexual purity. Purity is not just a word for girls; it's a word for guys too. We often stress abstinence from sex to girls because the consequences can be traumatic and life-altering for a young lady. But impurity of any kind, whether it be pornography or sex outside marriage, leaves scars on both young men and young ladies that remain through a lifetime.

"Keep thyself pure," Paul tells his son in the faith, Timothy, in I Timothy 5:22. Even though Timothy was already a pastor and had a good testimony and the confidence of Paul to entrust him with one of the churches, Paul still tells him, "Keep thyself pure."

Why?

I think we have the answer when we look at the city where Timothy ministered — Ephesus. If you want a description of the idolatry and wickedness of this large metropolis in Asia Minor, read Acts 19, especially verses 27 and 28, and listen to these Diana-crazed townspeople:

> So that not only this our craft is in danger to be set at nought; but also that the temple of the great goddess Diana should be despised, and her magnificence should be destroyed, whom all Asia and the world worshippeth. And when they heard these sayings, they were full of wrath, and cried out, saying, Great is Diana of the Ephesians.

Can you picture this crowd, not unlike some of our teenage mobs going in to see their favorite rock group? And you can be sure that where there is idolatry, there is also debauchery and immorality. In this setting, so similar to our own day, Paul instructs his son in the faith. Temptations lurked out there that could drag down even a

16

seasoned man of God. How much more a young preacher!

So what does Paul tell Timothy? "Keep. . . ." I love that word! The meaning is "to guard or watch over in order to protect from harm or injury." It may also be defined as, "not to let go of, to retain in one's power or possession." Wow! Put that in the context of what we are discussing.

Paul tells Timothy to always be on guard, be watchful, put up a barrier against anything that would defile or taint. Purity can be viewed as a rare jewel that you can either treat with disdain and cast aside or value as being so precious that you will protect it with your life until the time comes for you to present this gift to the one the Lord has prepared for you.

There is another passage of Scripture that we need to talk about when speaking of purity.

> *If a man therefore purge himself from these, he shall be a vessel unto honour, sanctified, and meet [fit] for the master's use, and prepared unto every good work. Flee also youthful lusts: but follow righteousness, faith, charity, peace, with them that call on the Lord out of a pure heart."* — II Timothy 2:21,22

Three things are mentioned here that will help a young person remain pure.

1. Flee youthful lusts

How can you as God's child keep free from contamination in a sex-crazed society? You can flee youthful lusts. You can either harbor carnal desires or flee from them.

Do you know that we need to be more afraid of the wicked desires that come from within than of the devil himself? We are told to resist the devil. Stand up to him! But not to youthful lust. We must run from such! Joseph fled from the charms of Potiphar's wife. Samson stayed around and toyed with his lusts. The one escaped. The other fell.

What about you? Do you think you are strong enough to be alone in a car with a young man on a star-studded night and not give in to your youthful desires? Many a Christian girl has deceived herself into thinking it could never happen to her only to find her life devastated. Don't trust the flesh — yours or the guy's! Run. Put as much distance as possible between yourself and anything that would fan your passions into a flame. In every situation, make plans beforehand that you will not compromise yourself.

2. *Follow after those things that will keep you pure*

To avoid putting yourself in temptation's way, pursue those graces that oppose the lusts of the flesh. Follow righteousness, faith, charity, and peace. Paul is saying that the best way to counteract the old flesh is to pour all your energies into developing your Christian walk. Perhaps you recognize these graces as being the fruit of the Spirit. Remember Galatians 5:16? "This I say then, Walk in the Spirit, and ye shall not fulfil the lust of the flesh."

Practically, what does that mean? Walking in the Spirit is daily living under His control. Staying faithful in your Bible reading and prayer. Cultivating a genuine, loving relationship with the Lord. Being sensitive to the Holy Spirit when He convicts you that something is wrong.

3. *Make friends of those who are pursuing purity*

You have heard grown-ups say, "She was a good girl, but she started running with the wrong crowd." It really is true. I know a young lady who became so lonely in her stand for what is right, that in a moment of weakness she threw away all her convictions and went over to the other side!

This story can be repeated over and over. Some girls have said to me, "I don't even know another girl in my school who is a virgin — *at least by choice!*"

But this is where all we have been talking about comes into play. You are out to please the Lord because you belong to Him. When you make that commitment to the Lord — to keep yourself pure — He will honor you. Pray for one, or two, or three other girls who will take a stand with you. Then, encourage each other, pray for each other, and make yourselves accountable to each other. In a few cases, there may not be any one in your school who will stand with you, but you may have a cousin or an older girl in your church to whom you could go. Perhaps your own sweet Mom would make a great confidant! The Lord will provide a way for you do what is right, I promise you.

I have a young friend who has kept herself pure. You can see it on her face, in her speech, in her demeanor, in her dress. I notice that young men don't take advantage of her. They respect her and long to be worthy of her. Why? Because that which is rare stands out. As Solomon said in Proverbs 31, about this virtuous woman, *"her price is far above rubies."* Rubies have great value because of their scarcity, and just so, both God and man put a high value on the rare jewel of purity.

Beware of Sending Mixed Messages

I want to emphasize again that purity is a heart matter. A pure heart produces a pure life, one consistent with what God has done on the inside. I'm sure you know those girls who put on a good show when they come to church. They look right; they dress right. But the things they talk about make it very evident that their hearts are not pure, *"for out of the abundance of the heart the mouth speaketh."* They still, very obviously, have defiled hearts. On the other hand, purity of heart will produce modesty.

There are two things that make for chaos, which is the opposite of *order* or *modesty*. One is a young lady claiming to be a Christian,

You can pick out a girl in a minute who claims to be a Christian but is really worldly. Her eyes give her away. And the way she stands or carries herself. She is telling you something before she even opens her mouth. One kind of girl comes across wanting to "hook" you. The godly girl looks on you as a brother in Christ and has an open, honest manner so you don't feel threatened. — B.D.

that a work of grace has been done in her heart, while her outward appearance testifies loudly to the opposite. She is claiming purity on the inside, but outwardly she is boldly declaring affinity with the world. The other is one who looks like a Christian with her modest dress, but a short time in her presence reveals that her interests are anything but Christian. She is a hypocrite.

Each of these young ladies sends mixed messages revealing a gross ignorance of true purity. The very definition of purity means "not mixed, free from impurities."

I gave the key to my wardrobe to the Lord when I died to self — to what other people thought, to pleasing the crowd, to needing to be pretty or skinny or in style. When I totally surrendered to the Lord that included how I dressed. After years of off and on struggle, I cared more what the Lord thought than what other people thought of me. — M.R.

4

What Does the Bible Say?

If you are a King's daughter . . . if you have been created to bring glory, not to yourself, but to Him . . . if you have been purchased by His precious blood at great cost and now are His and His alone . . . if your whole goal in life is to please Him . . . with a desire to do what He says . . . THEN you are ready to look into the Word of God to see His will for you in the area of your clothing.

Did you know that God Himself was the first Designer of men and women's clothing? That is a staggering fact in light of the argument people use that the Bible doesn't tell us what to wear. Even more astounding is the statement that God not only designed, but made the first clothing! We are not told how — if He used some heavenly sewing machine — or just said the word and it was done — but nonetheless, God made the first clothes. Here is what we are told in one brief sentence.

"Unto Adam also and to his wife did the LORD God make coats of skins, and clothed them." — Genesis 3:21

But we need to go back in the story to find out the how and the why. The very first mention of dress — or lack of it — in the Bible is found in the second chapter of Genesis, verse 25, which says, "And they were both naked, the man and his wife, and were not ashamed."

"Whoa!" you say, "Do you mean to tell me that the first man and woman created went around with absolutely no clothes?" That's what the Bible says. But we have to remember that Adam and Eve were innocent. Sin had not entered into the world. No evil thought had ever entered Adam's mind. Eve had never done one thing that did not please God or her husband. They were without sin.

Sadly, the account does not end there. Satan tempted Eve, and she sinned by disobeying God's commandment. She tempted Adam who willingly disobeyed the word of God to them, and through him the whole human race fell into a state of depravity. Since that time, every single person who has been born, except the Lord Jesus Christ, has been born a sinner.

Suddenly, the moment they sinned, "the eyes of them both were opened, and they knew that they were naked." Innocence was gone, replaced by shame and the desire not only to cover their sin, but to cover their nakedness. "And they sewed fig leaves together, and made themselves aprons." The word *aprons* has the idea of belt, girdle, or loincloth.

When God came down in the cool of the day to fellowship with them, they hid, ashamed to be exposed before His searching eye. What happens next is nothing short of a picture of the gospel. The first couple had lost their innocence and, therefore, their ability to commune with a holy God who cannot look on sin. In marvelous mercy and grace, God killed animals and formed suitable clothing to cover them. Oh, what a beautiful picture of the sacrifice of God's Son, Jesus Christ, to pay for and cover our sin!

> God used this literal event to teach us a spiritual truth. He replaced Adam and Eve's loincloths with "tunics of skin." Although Adam covered his loins, God covered him from his neck to his knees. This is significant: the work of Adam's hands was not acceptable to God either spiritually (his works of righteousness) or physically (his nakedness); only the covering that God Himself provided was sufficient for both. While Adam covered his privates, the Lord covered Adam's body. — Christian Modesty *by Jeff Pollard*

In our talk about modesty and clothing, the thing to mark here is the function of God's design. It was to cover nakedness, not only the secret parts (as Adam and Eve had tried to do), but as a coat would cover the whole body. The word "coat" used here in the KJV became known as an inner garment that usually extended from the neckline to just below the knees, or in many cases, down to the ground.

Clothing Communicates Something About the Person Who Wears It

In another reference to clothing in the Bible, God gave Moses instructions regarding the design of the priests' garments. The priestly coats, girdles, and bonnets were designed for glory and beauty. The linen breeches were designed to insure modesty of dress.

And for Aaron's sons thou shalt make coats, and thou shalt make for them girdles, and bonnets shalt thou make for them, for glory and for beauty. . . . And thou shalt make them linen breeches to cover their nakedness; from the loins even unto the thighs they shall reach:
— Exodus 28:40,42

A Baptist pastor from centuries past wrote concerning these priestly garments, "great care was taken, in the service of God's house, to preserve decency, prevent immodesty, and to guard against laughter and levity, and the like care should be always taken." [John Gill]

The priests were given a holy duty to perform, and the garments God designed for them commanded respect for that sacred duty.

There is a Right Way to Dress and a Wrong Way

The king's daughter of whom the Psalmist wrote in Psalm 45:13 clothed herself in dress that communicated the glory of her inward beauty.

The king's daughter is all glorious within: her clothing is of wrought

23

gold. She shall be brought unto the king in raiment of needlework: the virgins her companions that follow her shall be brought unto thee. With gladness and rejoicing shall they be brought: they shall enter into the king's palace. — Psalms 45:13-15

On the other hand, the writer of the Book of Proverbs warns young men to beware of certain types of women. Their wicked intentions are confirmed by their clothing.

And, behold, there met him a woman with the attire of an harlot, and subtil of heart. (She is loud and stubborn; her feet abide not in her house: — Proverbs 7:10,11

What do you imagine Solomon would think if he were to walk along our beaches today with all the show of flesh? I think that he would grab a lifeguard's megaphone and shout for all men to get out of there as fast as their legs could take them!

Clothing conveys a message. In the first case, the dress of the king's daughter reflected her inner life. The dress of the harlot advertises her business and tempts young men "void of understanding" to fall into her snare.

Dress to Impress or Dress as You Profess

If no other passage in the Bible dealt with God's will concerning our outward appearance, I Timothy 2:9,10 would be enough.

In like manner also, that women adorn themselves in modest apparel, with shamefacedness and sobriety; not with broided hair or gold, or pearls or costly array; but (which becometh women professing godliness) with good works. — I Timothy 2:9, 10.

Since you may be struggling with several of these biblical words, we will define our terms before going further. A good Bible dictionary helps us at this point to understand the full meaning of each word.

Modest: "kosmios" — that which has been harmoniously arranged or ordered so that the inner life finds its expression in the outward appearance.

24

Apparel: "katastole" — meaning "to let down"; practically a long, loose garment.

Adorn: "kosmos" — the noun form of "modest"; a harmonious arrangement or order , also the adornment and decoration. Elsewhere used to signify the world and its order.

Shamefacedness: "aidos" — opposite of shameful; a respectful and reverent attitude towards another. It involves an innate distaste of doing anything dishonorable; never wanting to bring outward disgrace; the opposite of shameless or having no ability to blush.

Sobriety: "sophrosune" — habitual self-control, with its constant reign on passions and desires.

We could stop right here. Having read these two verses, if you understand the meanings of these particular terms, you have all the guidelines needed to glorify Christ and reflect Him in your outward appearance.

Does My Outward Appearance Agree with Who I Am on the Inside?

This is the modesty principle. Remember, modesty is the outward expression of the inner life — harmonious, becoming and suitable. When the Bible exhorts women to dress in modest apparel, it is telling them to express on the outside in dress and conduct that which is consistent with the transformation that the Holy Spirit has made on the inside.

It seems to me a lot of Christian girls, even though they are not downright immodest, push it to the limit with slits up to their thighs and tight shirts or suggestively low necklines. They need to decide which side they are on, God's or the world's. Dress like a Christian or go all out the other way. — E. N.

25

Say to yourself, "Who I am — *a child of God who now lives to glorify God in every area of my life* — should be reflected in my whole outward appearance."

Remind yourself, "Is this true of me? Or does my mouth say 'Christian' while my clothes say something like, 'Look at me! I'm for sale — *cheap!*'"

I heard one man say, "If you are not for sale, take down your sign!"

Am I Out to Attract People to Me or to My Lord?

This is the holiness principle. Again and again in the New Testament, the believer is called a "saint," meaning "holy one." As a Christian young lady, you are aware that you have been set apart by God for His glory and His service. Remember how earlier we stated that glorifying God means showing others what God is like. If this is God's purpose, why do you find yourself so worried about following the world's standards in talk, tastes, entertainment, actions and dress? Your attitude should be one that opposes anything that would bring shame or dishonor to His Name, to His church, to His people, or to your own testimony!

Is there — *should there ever be* — such a thing as an unholy saint? Of course not. Only by being Christ-like can we attract people to the Lord. This is the whole force of I Timothy 2:9,10. Let's look at it again.

> *In like manner also, that women adorn themselves in modest apparel, with shamefacedness and sobriety; not with broided hair, or gold, or pearls, or costly array; But (which becometh women professing godliness [that is, god-like-ness or holiness]) with good works."*

Here Paul speaks of consistency in the life of the person who professes Jesus Christ as Lord and Savior. Modest apparel is consistent with a confession of true holiness. To dress extravagantly, immorally, or otherwise worldly is inconsistent with a profession of being a Christian.

Am I a Stumblingblock to My Christian Brothers?

It is time to talk about the boys — the young men in your life. There is a scripture that especially applies to this area of our discussion.

Be ye kindly affectioned one to another with brotherly love; in honour preferring one another; — Romans 12:10

"Dressing this way doesn't bother me!" some girls say. "It's the guy's problem."

Yes, it is their problem. I've had Christian young men say to me, "Mrs. Sheila, I have this terrible struggle with my thought life. I want so badly to keep myself pure, but it's hard. Even the Christian girls don't seem to realize what's wrong. The way they dress and the way they come across, it's like they are out to catch you. I really wouldn't mind being friends with them, but it's obvious they are interested in being more than just a Christian sister."

These young men were complaining about girls who were flirtatious. A girl can flirt with her eyes, with her teasing voice, or with a low-cut shirt. The word "flirt" simply means to tease with, "This is what I've got, but you can't have it!" It is to play at love with no serious intention. Can there ever be a time or place where it is right to flirt? Absolutely not! And boys can be as good at this game as the girls! The Bible says, "Let your yea be yea and your nay be nay" which being interpreted is, "Don't say one thing and mean another."

"But it's all just a game," you tell me. "I don't mean anything by it."

If you dress immodestly, you will get a guy who likes that sort of thing. The problem is that the next sexy girl he sees, he will drop you and go for her. When I think about when I get married, I don't want to choose a wife that every guy and his brother has seen half naked. — V.D.

This is where the love principle comes in. I have heard the comment, "That girl really likes the boys!" But does she? She flirts and works overtime trying to get their attention by the way she dresses and acts. But she does not love the boys. She loves herself! When she does not get the attention she is after, she goes off in a huff. Self-love is a form of lust, so easy to see in others, but sadly not so easy to detect in one's self. The truth is, if this girl really loved the boys, she would love them as brothers in Christ and do everything in her power to encourage their Christian walk. Not in her dress or her behavior would she want to cause them to stumble. The love of one Christian to another is preferential love, as our verse says.

What happens when you set out to get a young man's attention by flirting or flaunting yourself?

You may have already discovered that by dressing a certain way you can really get the boys to look at you. You can see them nudging one another and whispering. They may whistle or make some remark.

> *The first thing I notice about a girl is her face. I'm attracted to a godly young lady who tells by the joy on her face and the way she dresses that she is a real Christian. I also notice the people she is with and how they act. — W.C.*

Do you think they are admiring you? NO! Don't be so naive! They are admiring your body, the same way they do when seeing a picture in a magazine or in a film and find it sexually stimulating. They don't even have to know you for this to happen. It all has to do with the way God made men. In God's plan, the woman's body was made to captivate and intoxicate one man — her husband. But it was not His design that every woman who walks down the street do so! That's why women have instructions to cover themselves modestly.

The kind of Christian young man that you should be praying for will be looking for a young lady who is godly, one who through her life evidences the fruit of the Spirit. Where will he discover this?

In her face. That meekness, gentleness, joy and peace that are the evidences of a real Christian will shine through in her face. Her modestly clothed body will simply enhance, not distract from, those inner qualities that he respects and admires. He will then go on to study how she acts. Is she kind, generous, helpful around her family and in her church?

When he discovers those inner qualities, he will really want to get to know her. He will recognize that this young lady has put a high price on her virtue. She treasures and protects the body God has given her and is saving herself for the special young man God is going to bring into her life. Should He not, she purposes to live a pure life of singleness — whichever will bring the greatest glory to her Lord.

Think about it. There is probably a young man out there who is looking and waiting for that special young lady that the Lord is preparing to share his life. The Lord may also be preparing him to be your husband. I ask you, do you want other girls flirting with him and tempting him to sin?

I see so many girls, even Christian girls, getting their fashions and hairstyles from Hollywood. Let me tell you something. I'm looking for a girl who loves the Lord like I do, who worships the Lord like I do, who has the same kind of conviction on music, and dress that I do, who has kept herself pure. If I have to wait until I'm 75 years old, I will! I may have to pick out one in the nursing home, but I'm going to hold out!
— M.M.

Just as you want him to keep himself for you alone, he is hoping for a young lady who has not given herself away bit by bit to other men before she comes to him.

Be "kindly affectionate" to your brothers in Christ by praying for them, encouraging them, as heirs together of the kingdom of God.

Am I Glad that God Made Me a Woman?

This is the identity principle. God didn't make us neuter gender and then leave it to us to decide if we want to be male or female. God had a good plan when He made woman.

Until the 20th century, the strength of the true American women was their piety, purity, submissiveness, and domesticity. Women in the early days of our country had a definite calling — to preserve that which was good and godly in our society. They knew their first place of influence was in the home with husband and children, but their influence also filtered out into their communities and to the needy and oppressed in society. These women were happy and fulfilled, operating in the bounds of that which God had given them to do.

Sadly over the years, the picture of womanhood has so drastically changed that we no longer know who we are or what we are supposed to be doing. Even Christian women have lost their way. By modifying the world's standard, they strive not to totally neglect home and family, but in the end, they wear themselves to a frazzle trying to live in both worlds.

How did this happen?

I have read from several fashion history books to see how fashion designers explain the change in women's clothing in the last 75 years. Not only do these books show the change in clothing, they also show the change in women's attitudes towards the home and family.

> *Women's fashion lost its identification as a collective esthetic medium expressing women's feelings and qualities, but was seen as itself an endemic oppression of them, something generated by a capitalist and patriarchal society to enslave women without their knowing it.* — Sex and Suits *by Anne Hollander*

Translation: dresses and skirts — feminine attire — was seen by the modern woman to be symbolic of women's second-class citizenship in our society where women were stuck in the role of being wife and mother.

> *By taking up men's clothes and having them well-fitted to her feminine*

body, she [the modern woman] shewed herself to be interested not in female concerns like child-bearing and domesticity [taking care of home and husband] nor in the standard feminine uses of alluring submissiveness, but . . . the modern sort of sexuality customarily reserved for men.

Consequently, pants on women figured, naturally enough, in soft core pornography since the eighteenth century and they were often worn for seductive purposes by "fast ladies." — Sex amd Suits *by Anne Hollander*

That's feminist jargon, but what it means is that when women turned their backs on the distinctive roles set for them in the Bible, they voiced that rebellion with their dress. To make their way in a man's world, women started dressing like men. They laid aside their "meek and quiet spirit" talked about in I Peter 3:4, and became assertive and aggressive. The question was seldom asked, "Who is going to take the place of the woman in the home?" That no longer seemed to matter.

The world tells us that to be feminine, tender and submissive, is to be weak. That's simply not true. In fact, the very word "virtuous" used to describe the Proverbs 31 woman has the meaning of "strong" or "strong of character." Strong women of the Bible were tender and submissive. Consider Esther or Mary, the mother of Jesus, or Phoebe, a great helper in the church.

God is still looking for young ladies who will turn back to the Scriptures and model themselves after His blueprint for them.

But speak thou the things which become sound doctrine [teaching] ... That ... The aged women likewise [I guess that's me!], that they be in behaviour as becometh holiness ... That they may teach the young women to be sober [there's that word again, meaning "to have self control"], to love their husbands, to love their children, To be discreet, chaste [that's what this whole talk is about — chastity or purity], keepers at home, good, obedient to their own husbands, that the word of God be not blasphemed. — Titus 2:1-5

This is the specific description of the godly woman given to us by God. Woman is different and unique from her male counterpart in every way. In fact, the Lord wants us to delight in our differences even as He does.

Do you know that after several days of creation, God announced His work to be good? But after He took the rib from Adam and formed woman, He "saw everything that he had made, and, behold, it was very good." (Genesis 1:31)

I like to think that it wasn't until His crowning touch — a helpmeet for Adam — that God considered His work "very good"!

Let's be women who look like women and act like women, rejoicing in our uniqueness.

> *I guess I'm attracted to a godly girl because she stands out from the crowd. The way she dresses and the way she acts is so rare that I find it refreshing. The first thing I notice about her is her countenance. There is a glow and a spirit about her that make me want to get to know her better. — E.N.*

5

What Shall I Wear?

One girl said to me, "When I first started thinking how I should dress as a Christian, I looked around me at other women in the church and was really confused. Many of them had totally different standards and convictions from one another. They were all saved, and serving God in the church and yet did not agree on what true modesty involved."

Most older Christians well remember certain denominations who in the past held strict standards of dress. Many Christian schools still maintain standards like "No t-shirts with slogans on them." But we must admit, few pastors and congregations of our day are willing to address the question about what a young girl should or should not wear, lest they be branded as legalists.

Books on the subject are not much better. When I read books written by other Christian women seeking to help young ladies keep themselves pure, I heard them speak about glorifying the Lord. They quoted many of the same Scriptures quoted in this book. But in making application, each author differed according to the standard set by herself, her denomination, or her pastor.

One book was especially marvelous — so frank and biblical right up to the last chapter. The author ended her instructions like this:

1. *Project radiant beauty from the inside out.*

2. *Develop a pure and genuine aura.*
3. *Send appropriate signals and receive sincere responses.*
4. *Live joyfully within appropriate God-set boundaries.*

I couldn't have said it better myself. And yet the same author gave this advice to girls buying their clothes:

Look at yourself in the dressing room mirror when you try on a top and make sure it isn't revealing too much cleavage.

I ask you, "How much cleavage is too much?" Since when did Christian girls show any cleavage?

She went on to give this advice:

When buying pants, check that they aren't so tight on the buttocks or thighs that people can tell what kind of underwear you are wearing or when you slightly bend that your underwear (especially thongs) shows.

This lady is saying, "Just make sure your pants are only a *little* tight and that your thong doesn't show."

Since when are such items clothing for Christian girls anyway?

The Mirror of God's Word

God, however, has not left us without guidance in this important area of the Christian life. As we face this question together, we will do so by holding up certain items of clothing to the mirror of God's Word.

Though godly women whom you know may give you good advice, you must still answer to the Word of God. Remember, the real issue concerning dress is what pleases the Lord.

Look through your wardrobe for that favorite little tank-top you wear in the summer. Now, hold it up to the mirror of God's Word.

Does the tank-top cover your nakedness or does it reveal your nakedness? Remember, God's purpose for clothing was to *cover* the body.

So, look again at the tank-top. Does it dip too low at the neck or under the arms, or does it come short of the waistline when you bend?

I've seen girls having a tug of war with their clothes, first tugging at the neck because one or two inches of their cleavage was showing and then grabbing the bottom of the shirt to make sure their underwear wasn't showing!

Then they tell you they wear these clothes because they are comfortable!

Are you ready to hold up your t-shirts before the mirror of God's Word? I know I'll get an outcry over this one, but think about it. A slogan on a t-shirt across a guy's chest or on a baggy sweatshirt on a girl is one thing. A black slogan on a tight pink t-shirt across a young lady's chest, announcing "Daddy's Little Princess," is quite another! Can anyone honestly deny that it causes people's eyes to go straight to her breasts?

Simply put, most tank tops worn alone and many t-shirts simply don't pass the modesty test of Scripture. They are not hiding parts of the girl's anatomy that God says should be covered.

There are certain parts of a woman's body which need not only to be covered, but *unrevealed*. They are the secret parts that God has created for the husband's pleasure and for having babies! In all the fashion history books I mentioned earlier, no matter the period of time or the current style, these secret parts of the body were unrevealed.

Do we call a hat "revealing" or a jacket or coat "revealing"? Certainly not. The very expression means that we are revealing something that up until this time has been considered inappropriate to reveal.

In case you have become so blasé about modern styles, let's put it in black and white. Any item of clothing that exposes or reveals a girl's breasts, thighs, or crotch is off limits to the Christian girl.

A girl or woman who is willing to emphasize — and that is what you are doing when you wear certain clothes — her secret parts is showing off "all she's got" to any boy or man that passes by, instead of reserving herself for the one young man the Lord has reserved for her.

"Suggestive" is a word used for some styles of clothing. Next time your mom says your sweater is too suggestive, don't get mad at her. Stop and think. Ask yourself, "What am I suggesting?" An honest answer may help you understand your mom's point of view!

"Sexy" is another word thrown around to describe the world's fashions. You are told that the kind of underwear you buy can make you sexy as can a certain brand of jeans or make-up. Put bluntly, "sexy" means ready for sex. Unless you are ready to advertise such a message avoid the "look!"

Which reminds me — reach way back on the top shelf for that swim-suit. Go ahead, try it on. What parts of your body does it reveal, parts that as a Christian you have been instructed to keep hidden? Breasts, thighs, groin area jump out at you, am I not right?

Now, hold it up to the *mirror*. Remember that word, *shamefacedness* — meaning you should not want to cause others to stumble or to be tempted to sin? Can you see yourself parading up and down the beach or around the public swimming pool while still maintaining your Christian witness? As you look at yourself in the mirror, can you feel the smile of God's approval on you? Or, do you sense an uneasiness?

A pastor friend had just finished a sermon in which he stressed the need for young ladies to dress modestly. Afterward two college-age young ladies and their mother desired to talk with him.

"Is it wrong for women to wear two-piece bathing suits on the beach?" the girls asked.

The pastor replied, "If I were to knock on the door of your home tomorrow afternoon, would you answer the door if you were wearing only your bra and panties?"

In disgust the young ladies voiced their objection to the pastor asking such a question.

But he continued, "Have you stopped to think that you would be wearing more clothing with the average bra and panties than you would with a bikini bathing suit?"

The silent mother then spoke up, "You're right! I had never thought about it that way before."

I hear your objection. "But, I love swimming! Does this mean I can't go swimming anymore?" No, that is not what I am saying. But, it does mean that you will look for a way to keep your modesty in front of the opposite sex. Before the swimsuit became a fashion statement, men and women swam separately. With special planning, such an arrangement is still possible, especially if you get together with other girls in your church who have the same desire to be godly.

Now, it is my turn to get into your closet. What's this?

"But Mrs. Sheila, that's my favorite. You can't say there is anything wrong with that shirt. Besides, it's got long sleeves."

There is nothing wrong with your shirt — on someone two sizes smaller than you. Our Bible measuring tape says a "a let down garment." Translation: *not tight*. When the fashion is tight clothes, you have to buy bigger sizes. Here is where adjusting comes in. If, in your size, the garment is tight, get the next size. If in your favorite skirt, the slit is up to the thigh, sew up the slit or reject the skirt. If all the styles in the teen department are too short, go to the junior's or the petite's — or to the women's department, if you must.

I love the way my niece, Noemi, put it :

I like to look at shopping as a challenge. Finding modest clothes that are stylish takes more time, but I actually enjoy the hunt!

It's easy to have the attitude, "I'll never be cute and modest at the same time," but that's just not true. You just have to change your mind-set and be more creative. I look at an outfit and ask myself, What needs to be changed? Then I brainstorm and usually come up with a way to make it to my liking. I might add a little jacket or a t-shirt to fill in the low neck.

I find the more feminine and modest I look, the more positive feedback I get from the people around me. Of course, my Mom and the older folk like it, but you'd be surprised how many of my friends like it too. It's as though they find it refreshing! I like to think that I may be a trend-setter toward more modest clothes for my Christian friends.

Noemi is not only a great shopper, she's a Christian young lady who conscientiously makes decisions that will please the Lord and allow her to be a witness to others.

We don't have to cover every hanger in your closet, but I think you get the point. Every piece of clothing we wear should be examined in the light of God's Word.

Should a Christian Lady Wear Pants?

Thirty years ago pants on ladies was a controversial subject, both in the pulpit and in the pew. That is no longer the case. The average Christian grandmother, mother, and daughter all view pants in any style as acceptable. But, does that make it acceptable to God?

Look again into God's mirror. Deuteronomy 22:5 says, "The woman shall not wear that which pertaineth unto a man, neither shall a man put on a woman's garment: for all that do so are *abomination unto the LORD thy God.*"

A number of things in the Old Testament were called an abomination to God, meaning that God detested them. Examples are found in Proverbs 6:16-19. God detests a proud look, a lying tongue, hands that shed innocent blood, etc.

Generally, however, this word was used in forbidding gross moral sins. Throughout Deuteronomy we have many of these things listed:

1. *Idolatry — Deuteronomy 7:25*
2. *Human sacrifices — Deuteronomy 12:31*
3. *Witchcraft — Deuteronomy 18:10-12*
4. *Women wearing that which pertains to a man and men wearing women's garments — Deuteronomy 22:5*

The next question is, Are pants clothing that pertain to men? Many Christian women argue that pants have become so accepted in our culture for both men and women that they can no longer be considered exclusively for males.

Note the verse does not say "men's clothing." Instead it says "that which pertains to a man." "Pertains to a man" means that which is characteristic of a man. You might buy your pants in a woman's department, but they are still characteristic of men. If you doubt me, look at the figure on the doors of men's public restrooms.

Where's that mirror? We really need it here. One of the biblical principles we pointed out earlier was that of distinction. All the biblical instruction bears on this thought. Women are to be distinct from men in every way, including in how they dress.

Why else would this verse be stuck in the middle of Deuteronomy? All of the above offenses called an abomination to God were part of God's moral law, not ceremonial law. The ceremonial law was done away with when Christ came and died, but the moral law still governs our lives today. All of the above named sins are still sin and an abomination to the Lord.

Ask yourself, "If lying, murder, and idolatry are still an abomination today to God, has He changed His mind about this one thing — men and women cross-dressing?"

Pants on women not only breaks the identity principle but the holiness principle. Most pants reveal a woman's secret parts, that is, they reveal her crotch, especially when she is sitting. In many cases where the pants are tight, the woman's thighs front and back are boldly outlined. God calls making "bare the leg" and "uncovering the thigh," nakedness and shame (Isaiah 47:2,3). This includes shorts

What settled the pants issue with me is when I read Isaiah 47:2 where it says that if the thighs are not covered, the Bible considers it nakedness. Then I coupled this with I Timothy 2:9 and the word, "apparel" which describes women's clothes should be a long, loose garment. To me this means clothes must be knee length or longer and loose fitting. I just don't see how that includes pants. — N.S.

and even most pants. In such clothes girls may get stared at by the guys, but for all the wrong reasons!

Picture this. What if you arrived at school one morning and a guy in your class showed up in a skirt and girlie top and a handbag over his shoulder.

"Gross!" you'd say, or maybe even, "He's sick!" You would be really offended and rightly so. But why?

"But that's what girls wear?" would be your answer.

Think about it. What is the difference when you show up in a pair of jeans and t-shirt that is typical of what guys wear? They should be offended that you have adopted their style of clothes. The guys should be saying, "Gross! That's sick!" The only reason they are not offended is that we've got used to one kind of cross-dressing, but not the other kind. But whether or not that's your reaction, it is God's reaction!

Fit In or Stand Out

Are you struggling with this issue? Nearly all the girls you know at school and church wear pants — the women, too. If you show up in your skirt at the next activity, what are your friends going to say? They will call you old-fashioned. You might say, "Nobody, I mean, nobody believes women wearing pants is wrong any more."

What is it about us humans, especially teenagers, that make us want to fit in? There's a mold that you can fit into, but it is a mold of the world's making. If you squeeze yourself into this mold of fashion and behavior, the world will love you and receive you.

But Romans 12:2 gives us God's will.

And be not conformed to this world, but be ye transformed by the renewing of your mind, that ye may prove what is that good, and acceptable, and perfect, will of God.

There is another mold we find in Romans 8:29.

For whom he did foreknow [that is the Christian] he also did predestinate to be conformed [or molded into] the image of his Son, that he might be the firstborn among many brethren.

Incredibly, if you are Christ's then God chose you in order that you might be molded into the image of and look like His Son! There's another verse in I Peter 1:14-16 that says the same thing.

As obedient children, not fashioning yourselves according to the former lusts in your ignorance: But as he which hath called you is holy, so be ye holy in all manner of conversation; Because it is written, Be ye holy; for I am holy.

That word "fashioning" is the same as the word "conformed" in Romans 12:2 and has the same idea. It refers to the act of a child of God putting on the habits, mannerisms, dress, speech, expressions and behavior of the world out from which God saved them! It's the believer masquerading in the costume of the world. It is a Christian young lady putting all her efforts into making sure she fits in with the worldly crowd when instead, her consuming passion should be her inner transformation — exhibiting the beauties of the Lord Jesus Christ in her life.

So what if you are different and at times are the subject of ridicule both at school and perhaps even in your church! How blessed to be on the same side as Jesus when He said, "Blessed are ye, when men shall revile you and persecute you, and shall say all manner of evil against you falsely, for my sake." Surely we really can't put this kind of ridicule in the same category as persecution, but as reviling, yes. Our Lord says, "Rejoice, and be exceeding glad; for great is your reward in heaven . . ."! (Matthew 5:12)

Being different from what the world considers acceptable has a high price. No matter how kind and thoughtful you may be, if you don't fit into the world's mold, you will be considered "odd." Even among Christian women and girls, it's a price most are unwilling to pay. What they don't understand is the joy that comes with pleasing the Lord. — C.N.

We have come to the main issue we spoke of earlier. Is Jesus Christ going to be the Lord of your life? Is He going to be the Lord of your wardrobe?

6

Dare to be an Esther

Have you ever stopped to think about Esther? I have been reading her story recently in my Bible reading and was struck again how up-to-date her lesson is to young women. No doubt, Esther was beautiful enough to gain the attention of the messengers from the palace. "Fair and beautiful" the Bible describes her.

But why did the king choose Esther to be queen? What was it about her that made her a choice wife for a king? The historian Josephus writes that as many as 400 young ladies comprised this group from which would come the new queen — all of them obviously beautiful.

So what was particularly special about this young Jewish maiden?

The theme of the Book of Esther is *God's providence in the affairs of men.* Up until now, I understood that King Ahasuerus chose Esther because that was part of God's plan to save His people, the Jews. You remember the story. This mighty king of Persia who even ruled the people of Babylon, including the Jews brought by the Babylonians as captives from Jerusalem, was a very proud and powerful man. When, in front of all his peers, Queen Vashti flatly refused his request to present herself before them all, King Ahasuerus was advised to send her away and find himself a new queen. That is exactly what he did.

Messengers searched throughout the realm for the most beautiful women to present to the king. Knowing the authority of Persian kings where the king always got exactly what he wanted, I doubt these women had any say so in the matter. They were taken to the palace to wait their turn to stand before the king.

And that is where Esther enters the story. When she arrived at the palace, the Bible says that she found favor in the eyes of the keeper of the women, Hegai. For some reason he gave Esther certain advantages above and beyond those of the other women — seven attendants to wait on her night and day, special spices and ointments to enhance her beauty and the best part of the house of the women.

After twelve months of preparation, the day finally arrived for Esther to appear before King Ahasuerus. Esther found grace and favor in his sight, and he loved her. He placed the royal crown on her head, making her queen over the Persian Empire. In this position, God used her to save her people, His people, from the destruction plotted for them by their enemy, Haman.

But every time I have read this story, I wondered what set Esther apart from all the other women. Yes, God planned it that way. But, humanly speaking, what was it that caught the attention of Hegai, and eventually the king? We find a possible answer in Esther 2:15.

Now when the turn of Esther, the daughter of Abihail the uncle of Mordicai, who had taken her for his daughter, was come to go in unto the king, she required nothing but what Hegai the king's chamberlain, the keeper of the women, appointed. And Esther obtained favour in the sight of all them that looked upon her.

Only in one place does the Bible mention the beauty of Esther. However, the favor, or grace, she found wherever she went is much more evident. For instance, as soon as she was brought to the king's house and put under the care of Hegai, keeper of the women, he noticed her. The Bible says, she "pleased him, and she obtained kindness of him." Later the Scriptures say that "he preferred her and her maids unto the best place of the house of the women."

Instead of fitting in and blending in with all the other women, Esther stood out. There was something unique about her. I have concluded that her uniqueness was her spirit.

Now when the turn of Esther . . . was come to go in unto the king, she required nothing but what Hegai the king's chamberlain, the keeper of the women, appointed. . . .

Just this one statement shows that she was not a vain, grasping sort of person, but of a meek and submissive spirit. Hopefully I am not stretching my imagination too far when I picture her as being a loving, giving sort of person, not thinking so much of herself as of others. Perhaps God had used her in that strange environment to comfort lonely girls far away from their homes, to listen to sad stories of distress from girls who had no one else to turn to. No wonder Hegai favored her!

As I read, I found another key to understanding her amazing spirit — *her up-bringing.* The Scriptures describe Esther's relationship with Mordecai, her older cousin, this way in Esther 2:7:

And he brought up Hadassah, that is, Esther, his uncle's daughter: for she had neither father nor mother . . . whom Mordecai, when her father and mother were dead, took for his own daughter.

The words, "brought up" have the idea of "nursing, nurturing, nourishing faithfully and steadily." Esther's family was carried away from Jerusalem by Nebuchadnezzar, king of Babylon, to a country that knew not the ways of the Jews nor the God of the Jews.

In this environment, Mordecai "brought up" Esther, teaching her the ways of her father and mother and their God. Certainly, he told her the stories of how God had chosen the people of Israel to be His people in order that they might show to the nations around them the glories of the living and the true God. Mordecai would tell her the story of Israel's deliverance from Egypt and the miraculous crossing of the Red Sea, the commandments given at Mount Sinai, and the victories God gave them in the promised land.

Doubtless, Esther had herself come to trust this Sovereign God who had faithfully kept His Word to His people. She saw herself as one set aside by the living God to be a witness in a strange and pagan country. Mordecai may have even told her of the prophet Isaiah's promise, that if they would serve the Lord and not join themselves to idols that God would again bring them to their own land.

If all this is true and I have to believe it to be so, then this explains Esther's spirit. She was God's ambassador in the palace. The fact she belonged to Him set her apart from everyone else, not only in her own eyes, but also in the eyes of everyone who became acquainted with her.

And Esther obtained favour in the sight of all them that looked upon her.

She found grace in their sight. Her beautiful spirit caused them to think well of her.

The story goes on in Esther 2:16-17.

So Esther was taken unto king Ahasuerus into his house royal . . . And the king loved Esther above all the women, and she obtained grace and favour in his sight more than all the virgins; so that he set the royal crown upon her head and made her queen instead of Vashti.

Even the king saw something different in Esther. Finally, he had found someone worthy to sit beside him as queen. I'm sure that a wholesomeness, an attractive modesty and sweetness, set our Jewish heroine apart from all others. She did not need position to give her worth because she already seemed to know who she was and why she was there. Neither did she appear self-conscious in the king's presence because she knew her life was in God's hands and that He, not the king, was directing her path.

We have no reason to believe that Esther sought to be queen. We know that she was chosen by God and in His divine providence brought her to be the Queen of Persia. On the other hand, she did not sell her birthright for this privilege. She did not through worldly devices appeal to the fleshly nature of the king. Instead, he found in Esther two qualities that make any woman beautiful — *virtue and modesty*.

Because Esther was different and dared to stand alone, she was a mighty instrument in God's hands to save a nation!

Young lady, this is a true story, not an allegory, but if I attempted to make up an allegory to fit the message of this book, I could do no better than what the Holy Spirit has given us in God's Word. I challenge you, dare to be different. Dare to be an Esther!

7

Beauty

Is it wrong to want to be beautiful? Is the Lord displeased when we spend time and money on making ourselves physically attractive?

The world has its definition of beauty, but we know that kind of beauty is fading and often false — just a shadow of the real thing.

A famous model once said in an interview, "I am perfect, but none of me is real." How sad!

So what is true beauty?

The first mention in the Bible of the English word "beauty" is found in Exodus 28:2 where the Lord describes to Moses the garments of the high priest. These garments were to be "for glory and for beauty." They were to give dignity to the priestly office, but beyond that they were to represent the glory and beauty of our Great High Priest, the Lord Jesus Christ. This gives us a clue to the biblical definition of beauty.

Furthermore, Isaiah wrote, "Thine eyes shall see the king in his beauty." (Isaiah 33:17) And Zechariah wrote, "For how great is his goodness, and how great is his beauty!" (Zechariah 9:17)

We may therefore conclude from the biblical statements that God Himself is the essence of all beauty. His grace, mercy and love are all part of His beauty!

If God is the perfection of beauty, is beauty something He holds

Himself alone or does He communicate beauty to His creation?

Well, the Psalmist wrote, "The heavens declare the glory of God; and the firmament sheweth his handywork." (Psalms 19:1)

Have you ever caught a glimpse of a flaming sunset settling behind a cascade of mountain ranges? Or, have you ever hiked a trail through a forest of tall trees shading a carpet of bluebells that stretched as far as the eye could see?

Perhaps in the gentle smile of a little sister or in the marvelous design of a new baby brother's fingers and toes, you have seen a simple but awesome beauty that momentarily overwhelmed you.

Daily we see evidence all around us, sometimes even in the most unexpected places, of God's glory and beauty.

That which best and most perfectly reflects who God is, is true beauty!

In Ezekiel 16, the Lord's prophet illustrated this truth as He described Israel. In her original state, Israel was pagan, unwashed and unkempt and thrown onto the trash heap with absolutely no mercy from anyone.

The prophet said that the Lord passed by, saw Israel in her dreadful condition, and cried, "Live." And Israel lived. The Lord took her, washed her from her filthiness, clothed her royally, and placed a beautiful crown upon her head. What a picture of God's mercy and grace!

> *Thus wast thou decked with gold and silver; and thy raiment was of fine linen, and silk, and broidered work; thou didst eat fine flour, and honey, and oil: and thou wast exceeding beautiful, and thou didst prosper into a kingdom. And thy renown went forth among the heathen for thy beauty: for it was perfect through my comeliness, which I had put upon thee, saith the Lord GOD. — Ezekiel 16:13, 14*

Notice, why was Israel "exceeding beautiful"? Ezekiel says it's because God put His beauty on her!

"But what does that have to do with me?" you might ask.

"Everything!"

If you buy into the world's definition of beauty, you will spend the rest of your life striving for something almost impossible to attain, yet empty and passing if you should attain it.

How I pity the poor girls trying to look like this model or that movie star!

On the other hand, how saintly and well-blessed is that young lady who understands that true beauty is found in the life of the one being conformed to the image of Jesus Christ! That is what all girls should want to look like. That is a beauty accessible to everyone of us, not just to those who have perfect physical features.

Again, that which most perfectly reflects who God is, is true beauty. Outward beauty is only skin deep and fades quickly. The young lady who is after God's own heart is concerned with cultivating that inner beauty of spirit.

The Psalmist said, "The king's daughter is all glorious within: her clothing is of wrought gold." (Psalm 45:13) Yes, she is dressed elegantly, but her true beauty is found in the glow of godliness that shines from within.

How do you obtain this beauty? Does it have anything to do with cosmetics, clothes or hairstyles?

> *We all want to be attractive and pretty. Many times the prevailing idea is that one has to be seductive to be attractive. Even though Christian girls know its wrong, they go along so they will be thought pretty or cool and will be accepted. — A.F.*

Of course not! Though you were to have a complete cosmetic makeover that would make others stop in stunned amazement as they gaze at your outward beauty, it is nothing compared to the inner beauty of a holy life.

Makeovers take an hour or two to complete. Inner beauty takes a lifetime. It begins when you become a Christian and progresses as you learn to read God's Word and spend time in His presence. You learn to love His Word and seek out His instructions on how to live the Christian life.

If you spend thirty minutes a day preening your outward appearance, you need to spend more time cultivating this inner beauty.

When the Psalmist said, "Worship the LORD in the beauty of holiness" (Psalm 29:2), I believe he spoke of worshipping God in the beauty of HIS holiness. The verse proves that there is beauty in holiness, and I believe it implies that there is beauty even in *our* holiness.

I am convinced that true beauty is when all that is beautiful in Christ is evidenced in His child. That places beauty within the reach of every child of God!

My mother was an excellent example of the beauty of holiness. She spent her life as a missionary wife on the road with my missionary dad, living sacrificially, seldom having a minute to think of herself. By no stretch of the imagination would she have been considered beautiful in the eyes of the world. However, to this day, when I think of her, I remember those times she came from her early morning communion with the Lord to get me ready for school. An indescribable radiance on her face transformed her into the most beautiful woman I have ever seen. In those moments, it was if I caught a glimpse of Christ Himself!

Now, that's the "beauty of holiness!"

When we speak of the beauty of holiness, are we suggesting that girls go around neglecting their outward appearance? Not at all. Though some young ladies do seem to think that in order to be

Whenever a guy looks at me, I pray that he sees Christ first reflected in me. Recently I have prayed that I might decrease and He might increase in my life. It's not easy because I, like most girls, long for a husband and marriage, but if a young man is not attracted to me because of my spiritual qualities, then he is not the Lord's choice for me. — B.J.

spiritual they must look unkempt or drab. It's a shame, but other girls tell me that is what puts them off from seeking to know what the Bible says about wearing the right clothes. They are afraid God will want them to look ugly.

Nothing could be farther from the truth. If God had loved drab, He would have made the skies a continual gray and all the leaves on trees a pallid brown. God loves variety, color and design.

> Consider the lilies how they grow: they toil not, they spin not; and yet I say unto you, that Solomon in all his glory was not arrayed like one of these. — Luke 12:27

How does God clothe lilies? Beautifully.

Elizabeth Handford described it this way in her book, *Your Clothes Say It for You*:

> It does not honor the Lord for a woman to let her hair straggle in lumpy, oily coils, or her slip show ragged, trailing lace. Unpolished shoes, with run-down heels and runs in stockings don't honor the Lord. A shapeless wrinkled dress over an obese body doesn't prove a woman loves God. . . . The Christian's body is the temple of the Holy Spirit. We dishonor Him when we abuse His temple.

> So when the godly woman wants her appearance to show she belongs to the Lord, she'll keep her hair gleaming clean and neat. Her fingernails will be trimmed and clean. She will use underarm deodorant and a razor when it's needed. She'll brush her teeth and make sure her breath is sweet. Her complexion will be as clear and fresh as a healthy diet and soap and water can make it. Her clothing will be clean and wrinkle-free, well-fitting and suitable. After all, she is a princess, a daughter of the King of kings and her appearance ought to honor Him.

Mrs. Handford wrote that book thirty years ago and some of her language appears a bit old-fashioned, but her principles are not.

I would go a step further. Go ahead. Discover the colors that look best on you. Pick a style that best suits your personality. Add an unusual belt or a piece of jewelry that gives a bit of pizzazz! As noted before, God loves variety and design in nature, so why should His children not love the same?

There are Christian ladies who seem to think that they are limited to jean skirts and jumpers. It's almost like a uniform with them. If that is what they enjoy wearing, fine. But biblical guidelines leave plenty of room for individuality and creativity. This is especially true when we are not bound up by what Hollywood or the latest fashion designer dictates. It's the worldly crowd that seems to be enslaved to a certain set of rules and is scared to step outside the box of public opinion.

> *I guess before that I really wanted guys to look at me and think I was pretty. It wasn't that I wanted to be sexy — I was a Christian and knew that wasn't right. I guess I was worried that if I gave it all to the Lord, I would have to wear clothes that made me look fat, or frumpy.*
> *— B.R.*

Praise the Lord, the Christian young lady is set free from the world, the flesh, and the devil, and she is set free from public opinion!

One of my young friends puts it this way:

Modesty does not mean giving up color, beauty, or even style. It simply means presenting myself in a way that glorifies God and not self. Many times a little creativity when shopping can lead to success when trying to find a modest outfit. I look on it as beating the system. Fashion designers tell me that I have to dress immodestly to be in style, but I have discovered that with a little creative thinking and determination, I can still look nice in a way that will be pleasing to a holy God. — B.R.

8

God's Army

I realize we have spent much time discussing dress, modesty, and purity. I long for young people to be modest and pure through and through. But that is not the only reason I would write to you. Some time ago, while waiting on the Lord, He gave me several promises. These promises joined together gave me reason to start praying that He would raise up a group of young people — specifically, your generation — to bring our nation back to God.

But not our nation alone. Being born into a missionary family, I have such a burden for the evangelization of the entire world that I would include in this hope that this same generation would then go forth and tell the nations His good news.

With these promises in mind and with what God has put into my heart to pray, I give you this challenge.

God, whose eyes "run to and fro throughout the whole earth, to shew himself strong in the behalf of them whose heart is perfect toward him"(II Chronicles 16:9), is calling out a select band of young people — *Special Forces*, if you please — to accomplish a specified mission in these critical days. Impassioned by a love for Christ and compelled by the claims of Christ, these young people stand alert and ready to receive their sealed orders from their Commander-in-Chief. No sacrifice is too great, no mission too dangerous to deter these dedicated recruits. Their motto is, "Endure hardness, as a good soldier!"

What motivates such reckless abandonment to the cause of Christ?

LOVE. Once enslaved by sin and the Wicked One, now set free in glorious liberty to live holy and God-honoring lives, these young men and women are devoted to their Lord and Master.

GRATITUDE. Rescued from sinful and empty lives, saved and indwelt by the Lord Jesus Christ, they would tell you that not even a long life of self-sacrifice and service could begin to repay their debt.

PURPOSE. Life has no meaning, they claim, outside of finding the will of God and doing it. They were first born and then "born-again" to bring glory and honor to their King.

What defining principles govern the lives of this special company? GLORY AND HONOR. But not glory and honor for themselves.

Not unto us, O LORD, not unto us, but unto thy name give glory, for thy mercy, and for thy truth's sake. — Psalm 115:1

To bring honor and glory to the One who sits upon the Throne is their highest goal and that which establishes their standard of conduct.

OBEDIENCE. To these soldiers, the Bible is the ultimate manual for all faith and practice. The Word of God is their Commander's instructions and therefore their ruling practice.

SUBMISSION. Leaving their own wishes and plans behind, they are ready to follow wherever their Sovereign leads. This means surrendering themselves, their own plans, their own rights and personal pursuits.

Glory, obedience, submission — these are the very principles that govern a worldly army. Should the Lord's Army require any less? This is the caliber of young people the Lord is going to use to fulfill His will in this period of history.

The question is not, Is God going to do this? The question is, Are you going to stand up and be counted among that number?

You can be the one who goes back to the Bible to see who you are and how God wants you to live. You can be the one to build godly homes that will influence the church and society.

God is looking for clean, pure vessels to do His work. Will you be in that number? Oh, how I pray that you will prepare yourself in every way to be a vessel that the Lord will use.

Girls, you are a new generation. I have great hope for you. Just as you have dreams for your future, I do, too. I'll share something with you. As I have waited before the Lord in prayer, He has assured my heart that my children and my grandchildren are going to know the Lord and make an impact on their generation. Not only has He assured my heart about my children and grandchildren, but He has given me assurance about my spiritual children and grandchildren. You are part of that promise!

9

"If Ye Love Me . . ."

I don't know what the Lord is going to do specifically with your life, only I pray for you that you will prepare yourself in every way to be the kind of vessel the Lord will use.

You may have read through this book and wished you could talk back to me. Here is what you may have been thinking: "I'm not into all the stuff you have been talking about. I'm saved and on my way to heaven and that's all that matters."

My dear girl, if you have no desire in your heart to please the Lord and obey His Word, no desire to live a holy life separated from the world, then I tell you earnestly that you are not saved and you will never reach heaven.

Follow peace with all men, and holiness, without which no man shall see the Lord" — Hebrews 12:14.

"But aren't you being legalistic? God doesn't care about my outward appearance. He only looks on the heart, right?" you may argue.

If someone you know dresses modestly, doesn't wear make-up or jewelry, has long hair flowing down her back, and looks down her nose at others because she thinks she is better than they, there may be a problem.

She may be trusting in all these things to be acceptable with God or acceptable to her parents or church. She may be hoping that if she looks like a Christian, she will be one. She may be trusting in her good works instead of Christ to get her to heaven.

THAT IS LEGALISM! Joy and delight will be missing because this young lady grudgingly is trying to keep a set of rules. Modesty and purity must flow from the heart, a heart that has been changed through the transforming work of the Holy Spirit in salvation.

In contrast, when a Christian young lady obeys God's Word from the heart, joy and freedom result. Like Christ, she says, "I delight to do thy will, O my God."

Faithful obedience to God that flows from a heart that loves Him is grace, the very opposite of legalism.

Could it be that you are no better than the person you call a hypocrite or legalist? If you are trusting in a prayer you recited or in the fact you joined a church, yet you have no heartfelt desires to go all the way with the Lord, then it could be that your salvation experience has no foundation. It's not the real thing.

I repeat. Christ's life within produces Christ-likeness, perhaps faintly at first, but Christ-likeness nonetheless, inside and out.

Jesus said, *"If ye love me, keep my commandments."* Do you really love the Lord Jesus? Answer truthfully, because your soul's eternity may depend on your answer.

Perhaps I am asking that question backwards. Perhaps I should first ask you another question. Have you ever seen the love of God for you?

John, the Beloved Apostle said, "We love him, because he first loved us." (I John 4:19) Think about it. The Creator of this world. The Lord of all the earth. God Almighty. The Ever-existent One. He loved sinners like you so much He was willing to send His Son to earth as the God-Man to pay the price for sin.

John tells it this way, "Herein is love, not that we loved God, but that he loved us, and sent his Son to be the propitiation [a spotless sacrifice to appease God's wrath] for our sins." (I John 4:10)

If God ever shows you such love, you will never be the same. If you ever see that a Holy God would send His Holy Son to the cross to take the place of a wretched hell-deserving sinner like you, it will be the most astounding display of love you will ever see.

The day I saw this love, I fell on my face before God. I repented of my sins, and trusted Christ to save me. His Spirit came to live within me and I have never been the same. From the hour I saw His love, I pledged my life to Him to be His and His alone. You see, love responds to love. I really do love Him because He first loved me.

Right now, ask Him to show you your sin that sent the Savior to the cross. Then ask Him to show you the love of God the Father that sent His Son to the cross. And ask Him to show you the love of the Spirit who calls sinners to repentance and faith in the Lord Jesus Christ.

Cry out in faith to the Lord to save your soul.

King's Daughter:

Would'st thou be fair,
Without – within —
Peerless and beautiful,
A very Queen?

Know then —
Not as men build unto the Silent One
With clang and clamor,
Traffic of rude voices,
Clink of steel on stone,
And din of hammer; —
Not so the temple of thy grace is reared.
But — in the inmost shrine
Must thou begin,
And build with care
A Holy Place,
A place unseen
Each prayer a prayer.
Then having built,
Thy shrine sweep bare
Of self and sin,
And all that might demean;
And, with endeavor,
Watching ever, praying ever,
Keep it fragrant — sweet and clean;
So by God's grace, it be fit place —
His Christ shall enter and shall dwell therein
Not as in earthly frame — where chase
Of steel and stone may strive to win
Some outward grace —
Thy temple face is chiseled from within.

— *John Oxenham*